Question Authority

Essential Inquiries for Smart Voting

Jonathan Koch

Table Of Contents

Prologue

In a world teeming with voices, where the cacophony of opinions often drowns out the individual, one action remains a beacon of empowerment: the act of voting. It is not merely a right; it is a responsibility that shapes the very fabric of our communities, states, and nation. Yet, as election days come and go, we sometimes forget the power each vote carries—the power to influence decisions that affect our daily lives, from the schools our children attend to the roads we drive on, to the very air we breathe.

This book serves as a reminder of the importance of participation in every level of governance. It is an invitation to delve into the intricacies of local, state, and federal elections, understanding not just the who and the when, but the why. Why should we engage in a system that often feels distant or unresponsive? The answer lies in the profound truth that change begins at home, and every election is a chance to voice our hopes, fears, and dreams for the future.

As you embark on this journey through the electoral landscape, we encourage you to ponder these essential questions:

1. **What issues matter most to me and my community?**

2. **How do the candidates' platforms align with my values?**

3. **What local initiatives will impact my daily life, and how can I advocate for them?**

4. **How does my vote contribute to larger movements for change?**

5. **What barriers exist that prevent others from voting, and how can I help?**

Together, let us explore the profound impact of our collective choices, reigniting the spark of civic duty and ensuring that every voice is heard. Because in the end, democracy is not just a system; it is a shared responsibility—yours and mine. Let's make our voices count

Unleash Your Voting Power and Shape Your Community

Building Your Community's Future

Imagine waking up in a neighborhood where the streets are well-maintained, schools are thriving, and public services are efficient and responsive to your needs. These elements don't just materialize on their own—they are the result of decisions made by local elected officials who shape the policies and direction of your community. In this chapter, we'll explore why voting in local elections is not just important but essential for building a vibrant and thriving community that you can be proud to call home.

Understanding Local Impact

Local elections encompass a range of positions, from city council members and mayors to school board trustees and county commissioners. These officials wield significant influence over crucial aspects of community life, including:

Education: School board members decide on curriculum, funding allocations, and policies that directly impact your children's education.

Infrastructure: City councilors and mayors make decisions on road repairs, public transportation, parks, and recreational facilities that enhance your quality of life.

Public Safety: County commissioners oversee funding for police and fire departments, ensuring your community remains safe and secure.

Zoning and Development: Local officials determine zoning regulations and development plans that shape the physical landscape and economic growth of your area.

Why Local Elections Matter More

Immediate Impact on Daily Life: Unlike federal policies that may take time to trickle down, local decisions directly affect your daily routines and well-being. Whether it's reducing traffic congestion or improving local healthcare facilities, local officials have the power to make tangible improvements swiftly.

Accessibility and Accountability: Local elected officials are often more accessible to constituents than their federal counterparts. You can attend city council meetings, engage in community forums, and directly communicate your concerns and ideas. This accessibility fosters a sense of accountability—you can see the impact of your vote firsthand.

Tailored Solutions for Unique Challenges: Every community has its own set of challenges and opportunities. Local governance allows for tailored solutions that address specific needs, whether it's promoting sustainable practices, supporting local businesses, or enhancing cultural institutions.

Cultivating Civic Engagement: Voting in local elections is not just about choosing a candidate; it's about actively participating in the democratic process. By casting your vote, you exercise your voice and contribute to the collective vision of your community's future.

Building the Pipeline for Leadership: Many of today's state and national leaders began their careers in local government. By getting involved in local elections, you not only influence immediate decisions but also shape the trajectory of future leaders who may one day represent your state or even the nation.

Getting Involved: Your Role in Community Building

Educate Yourself: Research candidates' platforms, attend candidate forums, and understand their vision for the community. Look beyond party labels to evaluate how their policies align with your values and priorities.

Encourage Others to Vote: Discuss local issues with friends, family, and neighbors. Encourage them to register to vote and participate in local elections.

Collective engagement strengthens community bonds and fosters a sense of shared responsibility.

Volunteer and Advocate: Beyond voting, consider volunteering for local campaigns or community organizations that align with your interests. Advocate for policies that promote equity, sustainability, and inclusivity in your community.

Stay Informed and Active: Stay updated on local issues through local news outlets, community newsletters, and social media platforms. Attend town hall meetings, join neighborhood associations, and contribute your insights to discussions on local development and policy decisions.

The most important questions to ask politicians running for local government office typically revolve around their qualifications, plans, and values. Here are some key questions that voters might consider asking:

1. **Qualifications and Experience:**

   - What specific experience and skills do you bring to this role in local government?
   - How has your background prepared you to address the challenges facing our community?

2. **Priorities and Plans:**

   - What are your top priorities for our community, and why do you consider them important?
   - Can you outline your plans to address [specific local issue], such as economic growth, education, or infrastructure?

3. **Transparency and Accountability:**

   - How will you ensure transparency in your decision-making process as an elected official?
   - What steps will you take to maintain accountability to the community once in office?

4. Policy Positions:

- o What is your stance on [specific policy or issue relevant to the locality], and how do you plan to address it?

- o How will you balance competing interests and viewpoints when making decisions?

5. Community Engagement and Collaboration:

- o How do you plan to engage with and involve community members in the decision-making process?

- o How will you collaborate with other elected officials, community organizations, and stakeholders to achieve common goals?

6. Financial Management:

- o How do you propose to manage the budget effectively and ensure fiscal responsibility?

- o What strategies will you use to fund and prioritize important community projects and services?

7. Ethics and Integrity:

- o How do you approach ethical considerations in your role as a public servant?

- o What measures will you take to avoid conflicts of interest and ensure ethical conduct?

8. Long-Term Vision:

- What is your vision for the future of our community, and how do you plan to achieve it?
- How will you ensure that your decisions contribute to sustainable development and long-term prosperity?

These questions aim to provide voters with a comprehensive understanding of the candidate's qualifications, priorities, values, and approach to governance. Adjustments can be made based on specific local issues and concerns that are particularly relevant to the community.

Voting is a fundamental right that empowers individuals to voice their opinions and contribute to the democratic process. It's important to remember that voting is a personal choice, guided by your own values, beliefs, and priorities. Whether you're deciding based on policies, candidates' platforms, or personal convictions, your vote reflects your unique perspective on how society should be governed. It's a privilege to participate in shaping our communities and our future through the ballot box, ensuring that each voice counts in the collective decision-making process.

Your Community, Your Voice

In conclusion, voting in local elections is not just a civic duty but a powerful tool for shaping the future of your community. By actively participating in local governance, you ensure that your voice is heard, your concerns are addressed, and your community thrives. Together, we can build a community that reflects our values, supports our aspirations, and provides a brighter future for generations to come. Get involved, stay informed, and let your vote be the catalyst for positive change in your neighborhood.

Utilize the following resources to enhance your comprehension of local politicians. Record their responses and reflect upon them. Once you have gathered sufficient information to meet your requirements, you will be well-equipped to make an informed decision that aligns with your interes

Here is a list of 20 questions everyone should ask politicians running for local government office.

What specific experience do you have that prepares you for this role in local government?

____

____

____

____

____

How do you plan to address [specific local issue], and what steps will you take to implement your plan?

____

____

____

____

____

How will you ensure transparency and accountability in your decision-making process?

____

____

____

____

____

What are your priorities for improving [specific aspect of the community], and how do you intend to fund these initiatives?

____

____

____

____

____

How do you plan to foster economic growth and job creation in our community?

____

____

____

____

____

____

What is your stance on [specific policy or issue relevant to the locality?

____

____

____

____

____

____

What measures will you take to address environmental concerns or promote sustainability locally?

____

____

____

____

____

How do you intend to collaborate with other elected officials and community stakeholders to achieve your goals?

____

____

____

____

____

What is your plan to improve infrastructure (e.g., roads, public transportation, utilities) in our area?

____

____

____

____

____

____

How will you support local businesses and encourage entrepreneurship?

____

____

____

____

____

What is your approach to addressing affordable housing issues in our community?

____

____

____

____

____

____

How will you prioritize and support education and youth development programs?

____

____

____

____

____

____

What strategies do you propose to improve public safety and reduce crime?

How do you plan to address healthcare accessibility and affordability locally?

What steps will you take to ensure fair and inclusive governance that represents all members of our community?

____

____

____

____

____

____

How will you manage the budget and ensure fiscal responsibility as an elected official?

____

____

____

____

____

____

What is your position on taxes and fees, and how do you propose to balance the budget without burdening taxpayers?

____

____

____

____

____

____

How will you address concerns related to community diversity and inclusion?

____

____

____

____

____

How do you plan to handle emergencies or unexpected crises affecting our community?

____

____

____

____

____

Can you provide examples of successful initiatives or policies you have championed in the past that demonstrate your ability to lead effectively?

____

____

____

____

____

____

What is your honest assessment of our community?

____

____

____

____

____

____

Unleash Your Influence and Command Change

A Pathway to Personal Impact

Voting in state elections is absolutely vital because state governments wield immense power in shaping our daily lives and influencing national policies. Think about it—state legislatures and governors make critical decisions on crucial matters like education funding, healthcare access, environmental regulations, and infrastructure development. These decisions directly impact our communities, affecting everything from our children's education to the quality of our healthcare and the state of our environment.

But it doesn't stop there. These elected officials also play a pivotal role in how elections are conducted, in redrawing district lines, and in enacting laws specific to our state that can sometimes deviate significantly from federal guidelines. By participating in state elections, you have the power to choose leaders who truly represent your values and priorities. This ensures that the issues that matter most to you—whether it's better schools, affordable healthcare, a cleaner environment, or safer communities—are given the attention they deserve.

Your vote in state elections is not just about local issues; it's about influencing the direction of our entire nation. It's about making sure that your voice is heard loud and clear in the broader national debates that shape our country's future. Every single vote counts and has the potential to make a real difference in our democracy. So, don't underestimate the power you hold as a voter in state elections—your vote is your voice, your choice, and your opportunity to shape the policies and direction of our country for the better.

Policy Vision: What are your top three priorities for our state, and how do you plan to address them?

Budget and Spending: How do you plan to balance the state budget while ensuring essential services are funded adequately?

Education: What initiatives do you propose to improve our state's education system, from K-12 through higher education?

Healthcare: How will you address healthcare affordability and accessibility for residents of our state?

Economic Development: What strategies will you implement to attract new businesses and create more jobs in our state?

____

____

____

____

____

Infrastructure: How do you plan to address the infrastructure needs of our state, including transportation and utilities?

____

____

____

____

____

Environment: What measures will you take to protect our state's natural resources and address environmental challenges?

____

____

____

____

____

Taxes: Do you plan to change state taxes, and if so, how will these changes affect residents and businesses?

____

____

____

____

____

Criminal Justice: What reforms do you support to improve our state's criminal justice system and enhance public safety?

____

____

____

____

____

____

Housing: How will you address housing affordability and availability issues in our state?

____

____

____

____

____

____

Social Services: How will you support vulnerable populations such as the elderly, veterans, and those with disabilities?

____

____

____

____

____

____

Technology and Innovation: What are your plans to foster technological innovation and digital infrastructure in our state?

____

____

____

____

____

____

Emergency Preparedness: How do you plan to improve our state's readiness for natural disasters and emergencies?

____

____

____

____

____

Government Transparency: What steps will you take to ensure transparency and accountability in state government?

____

____

____

____

____

Energy Policy: What is your vision for our state's energy future, including renewable energy and sustainability?

____

____

____

____

____

____

Rural and Urban Balance: How will you ensure policies benefit both rural and urban communities in our state?

____

____

____

____

____

Community Engagement: How will you engage with residents and local communities to ensure their voices are heard?

Ethics and Integrity: How do you plan to uphold ethical standards and integrity in your role as a state official?

Collaboration: How will you work with lawmakers from different parties to achieve bipartisan solutions?

____

____

____

____

____

Long-Term Vision: What legacy do you hope to leave as a leader in our state, and how will you work towards achieving it?

____

____

____

____

____

The Crucial Role of Federal Elections

The Impact of Federal Elections

As we stand on the precipice of yet another crucial election cycle, the imperative to exercise our civic duty has never been more pronounced. The hallowed halls of Congress and the Senate are not just legislative chambers; they are the bastions of our democracy, where the ideals of freedom and justice are upheld. By casting our ballots, we safeguard the essence of what it means to be American—our right to participate in shaping our nation's course. Every vote is a voice, a testament to our commitment to a government of the people, by the people, and for the people. It is our duty, as patriotic citizens, to ensure that those who represent us embody our values and champion our aspirations. Together, let us honor the sacrifices of generations past by engaging in this foundational act of democracy, ensuring that the future we build is one that reflects the best of our shared ideals and ambitions.

In the intricate tapestry of American governance, none wield more formidable influence than Congress and the Senate. These chambers, pulsating with legislative prowess, are the ultimate arbiters of the nation's destiny. With the power to enact laws, allocate budgets, and scrutinize every facet of executive action, they hold sway over issues ranging from healthcare and taxes to global diplomacy and security. Their decisions resonate far beyond Capitol Hill, molding the economic landscape, societal fabric, and individual liberties of every American. As guardians of democratic balance, they embody the vision of the Constitution's framers, ensuring that the voice of the populace reverberates through every legislative corridor. Beyond mere governance, they possess the pivotal authority to impeach, ratify treaties, and orchestrate the grand symphony of American policy. Therefore, while the presidency garners attention, it is ultimately Congress and the Senate that wield the substantial authority to shape the nation's laws and policies.

As we prepare to cast our votes in the upcoming elections, let us remember that our participation transcends mere civic responsibility—it is a solemn duty to uphold the integrity of our democracy. Beyond electing legislators, these elections shape the composition of our judiciary and executive branch, influencing decisions that impact our lives for years to come. By engaging in this democratic process, we ensure that our voices resonate in the selection of judges who interpret our laws and cabinet members who guide our nation's policies. Let us seize this opportunity to steer the course of our nation, safeguarding the principles of justice, equality, and prosperity for ourselves and future generations.

What are your top priorities if elected?

____

____

____

____

____

____

Agree ☐   Neutral ☐   Disagree ☐

How do you plan to address [specific issue important to you]?

____

____

____

____

____

____

Agree ☐   Neutral ☐   Disagree ☐

How will you ensure transparency in your decision-making process?

____

____

____

____

____

____

Agree ☐   Neutral ☐   Disagree ☐

What measures will you take to hold yourself accountable to your constituents?

____

____

____

____

____

Agree ☐   Neutral ☐   Disagree ☐

How do you plan to handle conflicts of interest?

____

____

____

____

____

____

Agree ☐   Neutral ☐   Disagree ☐

What steps will you take to reform campaign finance laws?

____

____

____

____

____

____

Agree ☐   Neutral ☐   Disagree ☐

How will you ensure that lobbying efforts do not unduly influence your decisions?

____

____

____

____

____

____

Agree ☐   Neutral ☐   Disagree ☐

What is your stance on political donations from corporations and special interest groups?

____

____

____

____

____

____

Agree ☐   Neutral ☐   Disagree ☐

How will you protect civil liberties and rights guaranteed by the Constitution?

____

____

____

____

____

____

Agree ☐   Neutral ☐   Disagree ☐

What is your position on the balance between national security and individual privacy?

____

____

____

____

____

____

Agree ☐   Neutral ☐   Disagree ☐

What are your plans to stimulate economic growth and job creation?

____

____

____

____

____

____

Agree ☐　　　　　Neutral ☐　　　　　Disagree ☐

How do you intend to address income inequality and support economic mobility?

____

____

____

____

____

____

Agree ☐　　　　　Neutral ☐　　　　　Disagree ☐

What measures will you take to ensure fair trade practices and protect American workers?

____

____

____

____

____

____

Agree ☐   Neutral ☐   Disagree ☐

What is your approach to improving access to healthcare for all Americans?

____

____

____

____

____

Agree ☐   Neutral ☐   Disagree ☐

How will you address rising healthcare costs and prescription drug prices?

____

____

____

____

____

Agree ☐   Neutral ☐   Disagree ☐

Do you support any specific reforms to the healthcare system?

____

____

____

____

____

Agree ☐   Neutral ☐   Disagree ☐

How will you support public education and address disparities in educational opportunities?

____

____

____

____

____

____

Agree ☐   Neutral ☐   Disagree ☐

What is your stance on student loan debt and college affordability?

____

____

____

____

____

Agree ☐   Neutral ☐   Disagree ☐

Do you support any changes to current education policies or standards?

____

____

____

____

____

____

Agree ☐ Neutral ☐ Disagree ☐

What actions will you take to combat climate change and promote renewable energy?

____

____

____

____

____

Agree ☐ Neutral ☐ Disagree ☐

How will you balance environmental protection with economic development?

____

____

____

____

____

____

Agree ☐   Neutral ☐   Disagree ☐

Do you support any specific environmental regulations or international agreements?

____

____

____

____

____

Agree ☐   Neutral ☐   Disagree ☐

What is your stance on immigration reform and border security?

____

____

____

____

____

Agree ☐   Neutral ☐   Disagree ☐

How will you address the issue of undocumented immigrants already living in the country?

____

____

____

____

____

Agree ☐   Neutral ☐   Disagree ☐

Do you support any changes to the legal immigration system?

____

____

____

____

____

____

Agree ☐   Neutral ☐   Disagree ☐

What are your foreign policy priorities and how do you plan to achieve them?

____

____

____

____

____

Agree ☐   Neutral ☐   Disagree ☐

How will you navigate diplomatic relations with Russia, China, and Iran?

____

____

____

____

____

____

Agree ☐   Neutral ☐   Disagree ☐

What are your specific thoughts on our relationship with Israel?

____

____

____

____

____

Agree ☐   Neutral ☐   Disagree ☐

What is your stance on international trade agreements and tariffs?

____

____

____

____

____

____

Agree ☐　　　　　Neutral ☐　　　　　Disagree ☐

How will you address concerns about racial disparities in the criminal justice system?

____

____

____

____

____

Agree ☐　　　　　Neutral ☐　　　　　Disagree ☐

What reforms do you support regarding policing and law enforcement practices?

____

____

____

____

____

Agree ☐   Neutral ☐   Disagree ☐

Do you have any plans to address issues related to mass incarceration? And the enormous tax burden that comes with it?

____

____

____

____

____

Agree ☐   Neutral ☐   Disagree ☐

What is your stance on gun control legislation and the Second Amendment?

Agree ☐   Neutral ☐   Disagree ☐

How will you balance gun rights with public safety concerns?

Agree ☐   Neutral ☐   Disagree ☐

Do you support any specific measures to reduce gun violence?

____

____

____

____

____

____

Agree ☐　　　　Neutral ☐　　　　Disagree ☐

Where do you stand on issues such as abortion rights and LGBTQ+ rights?

____

____

____

____

____

Agree ☐　　　　Neutral ☐　　　　Disagree ☐

How will you promote inclusivity and equality for marginalized communities?

____

____

____

____

____

Agree ☐   Neutral ☐   Disagree ☐

What are your plans for improving infrastructure and transportation systems?

____

____

____

____

____

Agree ☐   Neutral ☐   Disagree ☐

Do you support any specific initiatives for clean energy infrastructure?

____

____

____

____

____

Agree ☐   Neutral ☐   Disagree ☐

How will you fund and prioritize infrastructure projects?

____

____

____

____

____

Agree ☐   Neutral ☐   Disagree ☐

How will you foster innovation and support the technology sector?

____

____

____

____

____

____

Agree ☐   Neutral ☐   Disagree ☐

What measures will you take to protect data privacy and cybersecurity?

____

____

____

____

____

Agree ☐   Neutral ☐   Disagree ☐

Do you have any policies in mind to bridge the digital divide?

____

____

____

____

____

____

Agree ☐   Neutral ☐   Disagree ☐

What is your plan to improve healthcare and support services for veterans?

____

____

____

____

____

Agree ☐   Neutral ☐   Disagree ☐

How will you address issues such as homelessness and mental health among veterans?

____

____

____

____

____

____

Agree ☐　　　　　Neutral ☐　　　　　Disagree ☐

Do you support expanding education and job training benefits for veterans?

____

____

____

____

____

____

Agree ☐　　　　　Neutral ☐　　　　　Disagree ☐

How do you plan to ensure the long-term stability of Social Security and Medicare?

____

____

____

____

____

____

Agree ☐　　　　Neutral ☐　　　　Disagree ☐

How will you protect benefits for current and future retirees?

____

____

____

____

____

Agree ☐　　　　Neutral ☐　　　　Disagree ☐

What reforms, if any, do you support for these programs?

____

____

____

____

____

____

Agree ☐   Neutral ☐   Disagree ☐

What policies do you support to combat substance abuse and promote recovery?

____

____

____

____

____

Agree ☐   Neutral ☐   Disagree ☐

Do you have any specific plans to address mental health services in relation to substance abuse?

____

____

____

____

____

____

Agree ☐   Neutral ☐   Disagree ☐

What measures will you take to support farmers and promote sustainable agriculture?

____

____

____

____

____

____

Agree ☐   Neutral ☐   Disagree ☐

How will you address economic challenges in rural communities?

____

____

____

____

____

Agree ☐   Neutral ☐   Disagree ☐

What is your stance on funding for scientific research and space exploration?

____

____

____

____

____

Agree ☐   Neutral ☐   Disagree ☐

How will you prioritize investments in STEM education and innovation?

____

____

____

____

____

____

Agree ☐   Neutral ☐   Disagree ☐

Do you support any specific initiatives for space exploration or climate science?

____

____

____

____

____

Agree ☐   Neutral ☐   Disagree ☐

How will you approach international trade negotiations and agreements?

____

____

____

____

____

____

Agree ☐   Neutral ☐   Disagree ☐

What measures will you take to protect American businesses from unfair trade practices?

____

____

____

____

____

Agree ☐   Neutral ☐   Disagree ☐

Do you support tariffs as a tool for economic diplomacy?

____

____

____

____

____

____

Agree ☐ Neutral ☐ Disagree ☐

How do you plan to address national security challenges and military readiness?

____

____

____

____

____

____

Agree ☐ Neutral ☐ Disagree ☐

What is your stance on defense spending and military budget priorities?

____

____

____

____

____

____

Agree ☐   Neutral ☐   Disagree ☐

Do you support any specific initiatives for veterans and military families?

____

____

____

____

____

____

Agree ☐   Neutral ☐   Disagree ☐

What is your approach to tax reform and fiscal responsibility?

____

____

____

____

____

____

Agree ☐   Neutral ☐   Disagree ☐

How will you balance the federal budget and reduce the national debt? Can it be done?

____

____

____

____

____

Agree ☐   Neutral ☐   Disagree ☐

Do you support any changes to tax rates or deductions?

____

____

____

____

____

Agree ☐   Neutral ☐   Disagree ☐

What reforms do you support to improve the efficiency and effectiveness of government?

____

____

____

____

____

Agree ☐   Neutral ☐   Disagree ☐

Do you have any plans for campaign finance reform or term limits?

____

____

____

____

____

____

Agree ☐　　　　　Neutral ☐　　　　　Disagree ☐

How will you address concerns about political polarization and gridlock?

____

____

____

____

____

____

Agree ☐　　　　　Neutral ☐　　　　　Disagree ☐

How will you address the impact of AI and automation on the job market?

____

____

____

____

____

____

Agree ☐   Neutral ☐   Disagree ☐

Do you have any plans to regulate AI development and its ethical implications?

____

____

____

____

____

Agree ☐   Neutral ☐   Disagree ☐

How will you balance regulatory requirements with the needs of businesses and consumers?

____

____

____

____

____

Agree ☐   Neutral ☐   Disagree ☐

Do you support any specific measures to improve workplace safety and environmental protections?

____

____

____

____

____

Agree ☐   Neutral ☐   Disagree ☐

Do you support any initiatives for student loan forgiveness or debt relief?

____

____

____

____

____

____

Agree ☐   Neutral ☐   Disagree ☐

How will you support lifelong learning and skills development in a rapidly changing economy?

____

____

____

____

____

Agree ☐   Neutral ☐   Disagree ☐

How will you protect civil rights and liberties in the face of national security concerns?

____

____

____

____

____

Agree ☐   Neutral ☐   Disagree ☐

What is your stance on voting rights and efforts to combat voter suppression?

____

____

____

____

____

Agree ☐   Neutral ☐   Disagree ☐

Do you prioritize judicial nominees who interpret the Constitution strictly as written, or do you prefer a more flexible interpretation?

____

____

____

____

____

Agree ☐   Neutral ☐   Disagree ☐

How important is it to you that judicial nominees have a record of respecting precedent?

____

____

____

____

____

Agree ☐   Neutral ☐   Disagree ☐

How do you plan to ensure diversity among your judicial appointments, including diversity of backgrounds, experiences, and viewpoints?

____

____

____

____

____

____

Agree ☐   Neutral ☐   Disagree ☐

Are there specific legal issues or areas of law where you will prioritize appointing judges with particular expertise or perspectives?

____

____

____

____

____

Agree ☐   Neutral ☐   Disagree ☐

Can you disclose the top sources of your campaign contributions and major donors?

____

____

____

____

____

Agree ☐   Neutral ☐   Disagree ☐

How do you ensure that your policy decisions are not unduly influenced by your campaign donors?

____

____

____

____

____

Agree ☐   Neutral ☐   Disagree ☐

Are there specific industries or interest groups from which you refuse donations to avoid potential conflicts of interest?

____

____

____

____

____

____

Agree ☐   Neutral ☐   Disagree ☐

Do you believe there should be limits on individual or corporate contributions to political campaigns?

____

____

____

____

____

Agree ☐   Neutral ☐   Disagree ☐

What ethical guidelines do you follow regarding donations and fundraising for your campaign?

____

____

____

____

____

Agree ☐   Neutral ☐   Disagree ☐

Can you provide examples of instances where you have acted against the wishes of major donors to support your constituents?

____

____

____

____

____

Agree ☐   Neutral ☐   Disagree ☐

How do you assess the current state of the national debt and its implications for the country's economic future?

____

____

____

____

____

____

Agree ☐　　　　　Neutral ☐　　　　　Disagree ☐

What specific measures do you support to reduce the national debt over the next decade?

____

____

____

____

____

Agree ☐　　　　　Neutral ☐　　　　　Disagree ☐

What areas of federal spending do you believe should be prioritized to address the national debt?

____

____

____

____

____

____

Agree ☐   Neutral ☐   Disagree ☐

Are there specific programs or agencies where you see opportunities for cost savings or efficiencies?

____

____

____

____

____

Agree ☐   Neutral ☐   Disagree ☐

Do you support increasing revenue through changes to the tax code to help reduce the national debt? If so, what specific changes?

____

____

____

____

____

____

Agree ☐   Neutral ☐   Disagree ☐

How will you balance the need for revenue generation with the impact on individuals and businesses?

____

____

____

____

____

Agree ☐   Neutral ☐   Disagree ☐

How will you address the potential consequences of a high national debt, such as interest payments and future borrowing costs?

____

____

____

____

____

____

Agree ☐   Neutral ☐   Disagree ☐

Are there areas of common ground where bipartisan consensus can be achieved on fiscal issues?

____

____

____

____

____

Agree ☐   Neutral ☐   Disagree ☐

How do you view the relationship between economic growth and reducing the national debt? What policies would you prioritize to stimulate economic growth while managing the debt?

____

____

____

____

____

Agree ☐   Neutral ☐   Disagree ☐

What measures will you take to inform and engage the public on the issue of the national debt?

____

____

____

____

____

Agree ☐   Neutral ☐   Disagree ☐

As we reach the end of this journey, remember that your voice matters—now more than ever. Every election, whether local, state, or federal, shapes the future of your community and beyond. By engaging in the electoral process, you hold the power to influence decisions that affect your life and the lives of those around you.

This book isn't just a guide; it's a call to action. Armed with the questions and insights within these pages, you can hold candidates accountable and demand the change you wish to see. Your vote is your voice—don't let it go unheard.

Share this knowledge with friends and family. Encourage them to join you in this vital civic duty. Together, we can build a more informed and engaged society. Let's empower one another to make our democracy thrive. Embrace this journey, explore the insights within, and spark a passion for voting that can inspire those around you for years to come!